CANADIAN CHARTER
OF
RIGHTS AND FREEDOMS

DEMOCRACY
FOR THE PEOPLE
AND
FOR EACH PERSON

By: Joseph W. Jacob B.A., M.P.A.

Order this book online at www.trafford.com
or email orders@trafford.com

Most Trafford titles are also available at major online book retailers.

Print information available on the last page.

ISBN: 978-1-4251-1153-3 (sc)
ISBN: 978-1-4269-8016-9 (e)

Trafford rev. 01/30/2020

Trafford
PUBLISHING   www.trafford.com

North America & international
toll-free: 844-688-6899 (USA & Canada)
fax: 812 355 4082

Also published by:

LIBERTY
PUBLISHING

British Columbia, Canada

TABLE OF CONTENTS

PRIORITIES AND EXPLANATIONS

Prior to 1982, Canada's written constitution offered rather little, in terms of guaranteed individual rights and freedoms. However, valuable improvements occured with implementation of the Canadian Charter of Rights and Freedoms. In the spring of 1982, the Canadian Constitution Act was officially signed by Canada's Prime Minister Pierre Elliott Trudeau and Britain's Queen Elizabeth II. This act, "ended the need for British approval of amendments to Canada's constitution."[1] Canada's, "bill of rights is called the Canadian Charter of Rights and Freedoms."[2] It became Part One of the Constitution Act and was officially put into force on April 17, 1982. The only exception was section 15 (equality rights) which came into effect exactly three years later. This allowed all provincial and municipal governments to bring their laws in line with the Charter. April 17, 1982 marked a momentous day, "when the Canadian Charter of Rights and Freedoms came into force, and when more than a century of hard fought freedoms became enshrined within the highest law of the land."[3] The Canadian Constitution is, "the supreme law of Canada. Generally speaking, all other laws must be consistent with the rules set out in the Constitution... This makes the Charter the most important law we have in Canada."[4]

Guarantee of Rights and Freedoms

A vital part of these prominent laws is section one, specifying, "The Canadian Charter of Rights and Freedoms guarantees the rights and freedoms set out in it subject only to such reasonable limits prescribed by law as can be demonstrably justified in a free and democratic society."[5] The key concept here is demonstrable justification. In essence, identifiable, measureable and demonstrable (or demonstratable) harm must have been produced <u>before</u> related punishment or penalty may be legally imposed. This fundamental principle of proven and truthful harm preceding legal punishment (demonstrable justification), "follows the model of international human rights documents, rather than the American Constitution."[6]

1

Legal Rights

During the 1800s, a famous father of democracy for the people, John Stuart Mill presented several classic democratic statements. Holding a dominant position in English political thought from about the 1850s onward, Mill was a clear, careful, considerate and consistant thinker. He, "learned that happiness in life is obtained by making it not the direct end. It is better sought by aiming at another object than one's own happiness: happiness of others ... followed as an ideal for its own sake."[7] When others are happy, there becomes a tendency for improved individual happiness. This is consistent with the colloquial, but seemingly reliable notion of, 'what goes around comes around'. If a person does nice things for society, sooner or later society will do nice things for the person. This concept also coincides with the trusted biblical direction of, 'Do unto others as you would have them do unto you'. In further support of this principle, another influential pioneer of constitutional democracy, John Locke describes, "There are innate inclinations of the appetite which are constant, namely, a desire of happiness, and an aversion to misery."[8]

Jeremy Bentham, a further founding father for the people, also expresses his views about happiness and democracy by explaining, "The art of legislation has two general objects or purposes in view: the one direct and positive, to add to the happiness of the community; the other indirect ... to avoid doing anything by which that happiness may be diminished."[9]

Regarding other important individual democratic rights, John Stuart Mill morally concludes, "the only purpose for which power can be rightfully exercised over any member of a civilized community against his will is to prevent harm to others... No society in which these liberties are not, on the whole, respected is free, whatever may be its form of government; and none is completely free in which they do not exist absolute and unqualified. The only freedom which deserves the name is that of pursuing our own good in our own way, so long as we do not attempt to deprive others of their fair rights, or impede their nonharmful efforts. Each is the proper guardian of his own health, whether bodily, or mental and spiritual."[10] This principle of fundamental justice is consistent with the Canadian Charter of Rights and Freedoms; when no truthful and proven harm is produced no related punishment or penalty may be legally imposed, because such action(s) are beyond the legal, "limits prescribed by law as can be demonstrably justified in a free and democratic society."[11]

Not only is it beyond the legal limits of Canadian laws to impose harmful punishments on people who have not produced proven harm(s), but this legal practice is also confirmed with the Charter's guaranteed right and freedom of liberty (doing nonharmful actions). Guaranteed personal Canadian rights and freedoms now include: the right to life, liberty and security of the person, and the right not to be deprived thereof except in accordance with principles of fundamental justice. Officially, these are called Canadian legal rights.

The constitutionally guaranteed personal right to life promotes, in principle, efforts for encouraging healthy human living, as opposed to destructive, harmful or death related actions to humans. This right to life clause is consistent with Abraham Lincoln's democratic principle of government for the people. Also, the greatest good for the greatest number and the greatest good for each nonharmful person are abundantly provided in the Canadian Charter of Rights and Freedoms.

The guaranteed legal right to liberty supports the concept that each person may do any action(s) that do not harm people or property. Throughout Canada, criminal offences ordinarily require, "proof of two elements, harm and fault."[12] In essence, when no harm is proven then no punishment is legally valid. Punishing (and thereby harming) someone who has not produced any harm contravenes principles of fundamental justice. A 1985 decision of the Supreme Court of Canada concludes, "A law that has the potential to convict a person who has not really done anything wrong offends the principles of fundamental justice and, if imprisonment is available as a penalty, such a law then violates a person's right to liberty under section 7 of the Canadian Charter of Rights and Freedoms."[13] Legally, this is a significant and

and fundamental constitutional right for each and every person in Canada, exemplifying democracy both for the people and for each person.

Also, the onus or responsibility is with the court(s) to prove guilt of harm produced <u>before</u> enforcing punishment. In Canada, people are presumed to be innocent until proven guilty; not the other way around. This, of course means that people in Canada are not legally required to prove their innocence in any concern relating to criminality. Respect and dignity for the person ensures that each individual is treated as though they are innocent until their guilt has actually been proven by a court of law. Naturally, this is much nicer and fairer than being arbitrarily presumed guilty and having to spend extra time, energy, and money trying to prove one's innocence. With the Canadian Charter, the benefit of the doubt is given to the individual (until <u>proven</u> to the contrary). Again, an important guaranteed legal principle here is that proven guilt of harm produced precedes related punishment.

Section 7 additionally guarantees the legal constitutional right to security of the person. This means each person in Canada is legally protected from arbitrary harm when that individual has not harmed any person or property. Security protection is compatible with the democratic right of being left alone if the individual so chooses. Consistent with this guaranteed legal right to security of the person, Mr. Justice Brandeis confirms and endorses individual security protection as he explains that the most comprehensive of rights and the right most valued by civilized man is, "the right to be let alone."[14]

Similarly, each person in Canada is legally protected with the guaranteed constitutional right against unreasonable search or seizure, as per section 8 of the Charter. Unless proven harm has been produced by a person, each person in Canada is free to be let alone. Proven demonstrable harm by the person must occur before that person (and related property) are harmed by legal search and seizure. In summary, legal constitutional principles here (with search and seizure) are similar to those for security of the person: proven harm precedes punishment; and the right most valued by civilized man is the right to be let alone.

Another guaranteed protection for the person is the right <u>not</u> to be arbitrarily detained or imprisoned. Again, demonstrable harm or quantifiable and identifiable harm must be produced by the person, before that person's legal right(s) are removed. In other words, people who don't do harm(s) are not legally allowed to be suddenly detained or imprisoned. Section 9 of the Charter provides this guaranteed right.

Many more guaranteed legal rights for the person are also now available. In reference to the Canadian criminal process, additional constitutional rights currently include personal rights relating to arrest or detention. Section 10 legally guarantees that upon detention or arrest, each person in Canada has:

10(a) the right to be promptly told of the reason(s) therefore;

10(b) the right to retain counsel, without delay;

10(b) the right to instruct counsel, without delay;

10(b) the right to be informed of the right to retain counsel, without delay;

10(b) the right to be informed of the right to instruct counsel, without delay;

10(c) the right to have the validity of related detention officially determined by way of habeus corpus (trial within a reasonable time); and

10(c) the right to be released if the related detention is not lawful.
The legally guaranteed right to be properly advised of the reason(s) for one's detention embodied in section 10(a) of the Charter, "is founded fundamentally on the principle that one is not required to submit to arrest if one does not know the reason therefore."[15]

In addition, section 14 of the Charter fairly guarantees, "A party or witness in any proceedings who does not understand or speak the language in which the proceedings are conducted or who is deaf has the right to the assistance of an interpreter."[16]

Furthermore, if any of these guaranteed rights are infringed upon or <u>not</u> officially applied, such cases are typically dismissed from court proceedings, because constitutional errors or omissions are unacceptable procedures that stain the judicial ermine. More specifically, section 24(2) of the Charter declares where, "a court concludes that evidence was obtained in a manner that infringed or denied any rights or freedoms guaranteed by this Charter, the evidence shall be excluded if it is established that, having regard to all the circumstances, the admission of it in the proceedings would bring the administration of justice into disrepute."[17]

Similarly, any person who is actually charged with an offence is not legally required to be a witness against themself. Section 11(c) clearly specifies, "Any person charged with an offence has the right not to be compelled to be a witness in proceedings against that person in respect of the offence."[18]

Also, any person in Canada who is officially charged with an offence has additional guaranteed constitutional rights:
1. to be informed without unreasonable delay of the specific offence, as per section 11(a);
2. not to be denied reasonable bail without just cause, as per section 11(e);
3. to be tried within a reasonable time, as per section 11(b);
4. to be presumed innocent until proven guilty according to law in a fair and public hearing by an independant and impartial tribunal, as per section 11(d);
5. the person charged with an offence to have the benefit of trial by jury where the maximum punishment for the offence is imprisonment for five years or a more severe punishment (except for military proceedings) as per section 11(f);
6. if the person is found guilty of the offence and if the punishment for the offence has been varied between the time of commission and the time of sentencing, to the benefit of the lesser punishment, as per section 11(i);
7. if the person is acquitted of the offence, that person is not to be tried again for the same offence, as per section 11(h);
8. if the person is found guilty and punished for the offence, that person is not to be tried again for the same offence, as per section 11(h);
9. if the person is found guilty and punished for the offence, that person is not to be punished for the offence again, as per section 11(h). This has important implications for people

whose jobs include requirements such as bonding or international travelling. As an example, any person who has completed punishment for an offence is legally <u>not</u> to be punished for it again by such actions as being discriminated against when applying for employment opportunities, particularly with people having criminal records for nonharmful crime(s). Such additional harmful penalty(ies) <u>against</u> the person punish more than once, thereby violating section 11(h) of Canada's Charter of Rights and Freedoms, the most prominent laws, and;

10. for any legal proceedings in Canada, each individual witness is protected with section 13, not to have any incriminating evidence so given used to incriminate that witness in any other proceeding(s). Again, the principle prevails of being punished only once for an offence. But, because of the important continuous legal quest for the truth, the whole truth, and nothing but the truth, there are only two exceptions to this legal right of witnessing. The first exception is in any prosecution for perjury (wilfully lying while under oath). The second exception is for giving contradictory evidence in any Canadian prosecution. Respect for the truth, the whole truth, and nothing but the truth is an essential and expected element in Canadian legal proceedings.

Fundamental Freedoms

Several more basic democratic freedoms are also legally available to all people in Canada. These guaranteed fundamental freedoms include: freedom of religion, conscience, thought, belief, opinion, expression, assembly, and association.

Freedom of religion legally allows each person in Canada to choose and practice the religion(s) of their choice, providing no related harm is produced. "The essence of the concept of freedom of religion is the right to entertain beliefs as a person chooses, the right to declare religious beliefs openly and without fear of hindrance or reprisal, and the right to manifest religious beliefs by worship and practice or by teaching and

dissemination."[19] Freedom of religion is intended to encourage
friendly and pleasant actions among all people in Canada.
Pleasant actions promote peace, order and progress. And, as
defined by the distinguished democractic philosopher John Stuart
Mill, "Order is the preservation of all kinds and amounts of good
 which already exist, and progress as consisting in the increase
 of them."[20]

   The constitutionally guaranteed freedom of conscience relates to
the individual's nonharmful freedom of choice, or the person's
action(s) of nonharmful free will. Also, "subject to such
limitations as are necessary to protect public safety, order, health,
or morals, or the fundamental rights and freedoms of others, no
one is forced to act in a way contrary to his or her beliefs or
conscience. Indirect coercion by the state is also protected
against."[21] Freedom of conscience is intended to promote and
reward actions that add value as opposed to action(s) that inflict
harm(s). Improvements in self esteem; respect for everyone; and a
peaceful society are some of the expected rewards. Also, all
Canadian governments and their employees are legally required to
produce actions relating to honesty and truth, the whole truth, and
nothing but the truth. Coercion by the state deviates from legally
acceptable behaviour, and can produce harm to unsuspecting
person(s). Coercion, by definition, is any form of compulsion or
constraint which compels or induces a person to act otherwise
than freely; it may be physical force but is more often used to
describe any mental pressure, such as duress, "which is brought to
bear on another's free will."[22] Coercion is similar to bullying, that
is, doing action(s) which harm those who are weaker or
unprotected. The Charter legally protects each person in Canada
from being bullied, either physically or mentally, by any and all
government employee(s), officer(s) and other representative(s).

   Guaranteed freedoms of individual thoughts and beliefs are
additional legal benefits provided by the Canadian Charter of
Rights and Freedoms. A significant purpose here is to ensure that
thoughts and beliefs, conveyed in nonharmful ways, may be done
so, "without fear of censure."[23] As John Stuart Mill explains,
personal freedoms of thoughts and beliefs require liberties,

"of tastes and pursuits; of framing the plan of our life to suit our own character; of doing as we like, subject to such consequences as may follow: without impediment from our fellow creatures, so long as we do not harm them."[24] Another essential requirement here, says Mill, is that, "Men and governments must act to the best of their ability."[25] Respecting these guaranteed individual freedoms of thoughts, ideas and beliefs, a senior Canadian politician recently concluded: "In Canada, we are free to think what we want, say what we want, and lead the lives we want."[26]

Freedom of opinion is another guaranteed right for the people and for each person. John Stuart Mill cautions that it is the duty of governments, and of individuals, to form the truist opinions they can, "and to form them carefully."[27] "Originality is a valuable element in human affairs. There is always need of persons not only to discover new truths, and point out when what were once truths are true no longer, but also to commence new practices, and set the example of more enlightened conduct, and better taste and sense in human life."[28] Mill further explains, "There are but a few persons, in comparison to the whole of mankind, whose experiments, if adopted by others, would be likely to be an improvement on established practice. But these few are the salt of the earth; without them, life would become a stagnant pool."[29] Examples of some people who introduced valuable improvements, including ideas and actions not previously popular, are: Pythagorus, Queen Victoria, Alexander Graham Bell, Florence Nightengale, Thomas Edison, Laura Secord, George Stephenson, Marie Curie, Abraham Lincoln, and Mother Theresa.

John Stuart Mill additionally points out, "If all mankind minus one were of one opinion, and only one person was of the contrary opinion, mankind would be no more justified in silencing that one person, than he, if he had the power, would be justified in silencing mankind... But the peculiar evil of silencing the expression of an opinion is, that it is robbing the human race; posterity as well as the existing generation... If the opinion is right, they are deprived of the opportunity of exchanging error for truth: if wrong, they lose, what is almost as great a benefit, the clearer perception and livlier impression of truth, produced by its collision with error...

We can never be sure that the opinion we are endeavouring to stifle is a false opinion."[30]

A similar truthful concept exists: if ten thousand people (or more) say a foolish thing, it is still a foolish thing. Large numbers don't automatically make it right. Beliefs and opinions are valuable resources assisting with improving living standards and happiness both for society and for each person. Choosing the best to improve the future is a primary purpose here.

Another important guaranteed freedom provided by the Canadian Charter, section 2(b) is that of individual expression. Freedom of expression includes: freedom of speech, freedom of the press, and freedom of communication in general, as well as any body gesture(s) such as a look that conveys meaning, or a showing of feeling. With this freedom of expression, however, is the consistent legal qualifier that the individual produces no related measureable, identifiable or demonstrable harm. For example, unproven or untruthful slanderous or libelous statements which can harm another person's reputation are not legally allowed. Neither is hate speech. The Canadian, "Criminal Code prohibits the communication of statements ... that wilfully promote hatred against an identifiable group."[31] Instead, polite and peaceful communications are expected of everyone.

In addition, section 2(b) guarantees freedom of other media of communication. Basically, this is freedom of communication in general, providing no related harm is produced. Other media includes communication forms such as telephones, radios, televisions, computers, fax machines, etc.

The Charter's guaranteed freedom of expression has a wide range of applications. This, "constitutional guarantee extends not only to that which is pleasing, but also to that which may be aesthetically distasteful or morally offensive."[32] Throughout history, what has been morally offensive in one era, has become morally acceptable in another era. The right for women to vote, the use of fireworks, and attending clothing-optional beaches are some typical examples. Freedom of expression is intended to improve communications within society. A constant quest for the truth, the whole truth and nothing but the truth encourages correctness and completeness of adding valuable ideas and related results.

Another cherished constitutionally guaranteed resource is freedom of assembly. This sociable democratic freedom is similar to the guaranteed legal freedom of expression, except such communication freedoms are applied to groups of three or more people, rather than to individuals only. As long as a gathering (of three or more people) produces only peaceful actions that do not demonstrably harm people or property, such actions and assemblies are guaranteed to be constitutionally legal. "Freedom of assembly has been seen as a form of freedom of expression, and under the Charter non-violent picketing has been held to be protected by section 2(b)."[33] Consistent with the Canadian Charter of Rights and Freedoms, in the United States, "The right peaceably to assemble is constitutionally guaranteed by the First Amendment."[34] Also, action(s) that demonstrate respect for rights and freedoms of others in society is a prominent responsibility of all legal nonharmful assembly(ies).

Freedom of association, a further Charter guarantee includes, "a collection of persons who have joined together for a certain object."[35] This freedom of organization or association, "is more than the right to attend a meeting; it includes the right to express one's attitudes or philosophies by membership in a group or by affiliation with it or by other lawful means."[36] Freedom of association is, "a freedom belonging to the individual and not the group formed through its exercise. It does not include a guarantee of the right to bargain collectively and the right to strike or lockout."[37] Collective bargaining rights including official certification and completing collective bargaining agreements (legal contracts) are usually separately negotiated among employees (including their representatives) as well as employer(s) along with appropriate government representatives, to ensure compliance with current policies and procedures.

In addition to legal individual freedom of association, the

Canadian Charter also respects society with the public good, known as the collective good, or the greatest good for the greatest number. Required association may legally occur for improving public goods or services. Demonstrable criteria including complete truthful facts relating to important concerns such as safety, timing, quality and cost directly affect legally required or forced association. Public goods and services (including related personnel) in areas such as schools, hospitals and roads are typically affected. "Forced association is permissible where combining the efforts of particular individuals with similar interests in a particular area is required to further the collective good."[38] In summary, as John Stuart Mill logically explains, "the democratic right of liberty for each individual, follows the liberty, within the same limits, of combination among individuals; freedom to unite, for any purpose not involving harm to others."[39]

Another guaranteed legal right for the people and for each person is officially provided with section 12 of the Charter, giving everyone, "the right not to be subjected to any cruel and unusual treatment or punishment."[40] Cruel and unusual treatment relates to behaviour that is not fair and ordinary being imposed on a person. Forcing an elderly person to reside and sleep in a cold harm-producing room is an example of cruel and unusual treatment. Encouraging a patient with constipation to eat large amounts of food, and then not allowing the patient to have enema priveleges is another example of cruel and unusual treatment. Witholding or preventing use of helpful and nonharmful medicine for a person is a further example of cruel and unusual treatment.

The additional guaranteed Charter right not to be subjected to any cruel and unusual punishment, usually involves any penalty being inherently unfair, or, that which, "is shocking or disgusting to people of reasonable sensitivity."[41] Imposing physical abuse or torture on a person is another form of cruel and unusual treatment or punishment. In the United States, as well, prisoners, "are still entitled to protection against cruel and unusual punishment by the eighth amendment."[42]

In fair constitutional democracies, the severity of the punishment is equated to the severity of the crime, or more specifically, the severity of the demonstrable harm produced. If little or no truthful demonstrable harm is produced then little or no punishment is legally allowed to be imposed. This fundamental principle has traditionally been represented by the revered scales of justice, balancing the severity of the punishment with the severity of the truthful harm produced (i.e. the crime).

Equality Rights and Freedoms

Equal benefit of the law is another impressive individual right guaranteed to each person in Canada. Equality implies that everyone is important. Respect for the person based on their actions of adding value and not producing harm to society is the significant legal issue here. Thomas Hobbes, another founding father of fundamental justice for all, explains, "Nature hath made men so equal, in the faculties of body and mind... From this equality of ability, ariseth equality of hope in the attaining of our ends."[43] A similar renouned philosopher, for the people and for each person, John Locke morally describes, "From the presumed intention of the Creator it followed that men were naturally equal, in the sense that no-one had more power or jurisdiction than another, and were naturally free to order their actions, and dispose of their possessions ... as they think fit, within the bounds of the law of nature which forbids anyone harming another or destroying himself, and requires each to try, when his own preservation comes not in competion, to preserve the rest of mankind."[44] In essence, equal benefit and equal protection from laws promote fairness for the person and for society. The Canadian Charter of Rights and Freedoms, section 15(1) specifies, "Every individual is equal before and under the law and has the right to the equal protection and equal benefit of the law without discrimination and, in particular without discrimination based on race, national or ethnic origin, colour, religion, sex, age, or mental or physical disability."[45] The Supreme Court of Canada has held that the primary purpose here, "is to ensure equality in the formulation and application of the law."[46]

As a minimum requirement of these equal benefit and equal protection laws, the Supreme Court of Canada has clearly concluded, "no individual is to be treated more harshly than another under the law."[47]

The Canadian Charter also received humanitarian recognition as being one of the first in the world to include disabilities (both physical and mental) in its equality guarantees. To enhance equality for everyone in Canada, section 15(2) of the Charter, "does not preclude any law, program or activity that has as its object the amelioration of conditions of disadvantaged individuals or groups including those that are disadvantaged because of race, national or ethnic origin, colour, religion, sex, age, or mental or physical disability."[48] The explicit benefit and protection here, "of programs designed to ameliorate the conditions of disadvantaged individuals and groups is intended to ensure that legislatures will not be discouraged from taking affirmative measures to enhance equality."[49] Trying to make a level playing field for all participants is an ultimate objective here. In summary, Canadian Charter laws include, "the notion that every individual is entitled to dignity and respect, and that the law should apply to all in an even-handed manner."[50] When everyone is treated with dignity and respect, and when everyone treats everyone else with dignity and respect, society is a safer, more secure, and joyful place to be.

Guaranteed equality rights also extend to human gender. As per section 28, all rights and freedoms contained in the Charter, "are guaranteed equally to male and female persons."[51]

Equality applies to voting rights as well, where each eligible voter in Canadian elections has only one voting right per election. No person in Canada is legally priveleged with two or more voting rights, because of apparently being more important. As per section 3 of the Charter, "Every citizen of Canada has the right to vote in an election of members of the House of Commons or of a legislative assembly and to be qualified for membership therein."[52] Equality of participation rights promotes fairness and respect for all, where everyone is valued as being important.

Mobility Rights and Freedoms

Mobility rights and freedoms of the Charter allow each person to reside and pursue the gaining of a livlihood in any province or territory in Canada. Essentially, sections 6(1) and 6(2) guarantee that every Canadian citizen has the right to enter, remain in and leave Canada, depending on their freedom of choice. In addition, every citizen of Canada and every person who has the status of a permanent resident of Canada, has the guaranteed right to move to and take up residence in any Canadian province or territory. Again, personal freedom of choice is a typical component in making these important geographic decisions. Also, the guaranteed personal right to pursue the gaining of a livlihood in any province or territory of Canada is legally provided with section 6(2)(b) of the Charter. Regarding these legal mobility rights, "It has been interpreted by the Supreme Court of Canada as guaranteeing a right of interprovincial mobility that ensures a right to move to another province to take up work there."[53]

Section 6(4) of these mobility rights also legally allows federal, provincial and municipal governments in Canada to assist economically or socially disadvantaged individuals, where the employment rate in that province or territory is lower than that of the Canadian national average employment rate. To actively encourage fairness and equality, improving living standards may be directed at areas needing it most. Such innovative incentives are intended to increase happiness and joy for everyone who adds value (and not harm) to society, particularly for those living in below-average standards.

Aboriginal Rights and Freedoms

The complete contents of the Canadian Charter of Rights and Freedoms also apply to all aboriginal peoples in Canada. Promoting fairness and having opportunities for adding value to improve living standards, aboriginal people also receive guaranteed protection with all previous legally recognized rights and freedoms, including those in treaties and proclamations.

More specifically, section 25 declares, "The guarantee in this Charter of certain rights and freedoms shall not be construed so as to abrogate or derogate from any aboriginal treaty, or other rights and freedoms that pertain to the aboriginal peoples of Canada including:

(a) any rights or freedoms that have been recognized by the Royal Proclamation of October 7, 1763; and

(b) any rights or freedoms that may be acquired by the aboriginal peoples of Canada by way of land claim settlements."[54]

Respect for all these guaranteed rights and freedoms is intented to improve living standards for everyone whose intentions and actions are to add value to society, with no demonstrable harm(s).

Language Rights and Freedoms

English and French are the only official languages of Canada. And, as per section 16(1) they, "have equality of status and equal rights and priveleges as to their use in all institutions of the parliament and government of Canada."[55] Improving harmony in society is a worthy purpose of any communication system. Effective and efficient communications add value and improve both output results and safety conditions when producing goods and services. However, danger and harms can quickly occur when confusing communications are produced. For example, if all pilots and air traffic controllers using Canadian air space were allowed to speak any language of their choice, severe demonstrable harm(s) could soon result. Such people simultaneously speaking English, French, Swahili, Mandarin, etc. could soon produce true confusions, misinterpretations, dangers and serious demonstrable harms. To improve public safety and security in Canada, only one language (English) is legally allowed to be used in air transportation and communications.

Additionally, section 27 explains, "This Charter shall be interpreted in a manner consistent with the preservation and enhancement of the multicultural heritage of Canadians."[56] Usually, in non-general public areas including private social events, preservation and enhancement of a multi-cultural heritage continues to be legally encouraged, as long as no related harm is produced.

However, for public safety and security reasons, involving improving communications, information communicated in public places is safer and more joyful if done in the official language of the area (Engish and French in Quebec and New Brunswick; and English in the remainder of Canada). One public language provides security without information discrimination.

When most people in an area are fluent in one language only, multiple public languages can quickly produce confusions, frustrations, accidents, rage, vulnerabilities, misinterpretations, and related truthful demonstrable harms. For example, when persons within a public domain purposely do not want other members of the public to understand certain verbal comments, they can start speaking a strange language. This tends to instill confusion, anger, fear, insecurity, inferiority, and inequality in the mind of the excluded listener. Why are they speaking a language which I don't understand? Are they saying something harmful affecting me, and I am unable to defend myself because I don't understand what is being said? This is rude, selfish and arrogant behaviour, demonstrating disrespect to another person(s). It is not fair communication(s) for the listener(s) who cannot understand what is being said. Neither is it equal benefit of the law. More truthfully, it is communication discrimination. Unchecked, it can assist with such harmful actions as terrorist activities, when the unsuspecting, vulnerable pubic is unable to defend themselves, because they don't understand what is being communicated. A little knowledge can be a dangerous thing.

Keeping it simple, clear, correct, complete and consistent for everyone in public places improves understanding, equality, harmony, happiness, order, security and progress. If it is worthwhile to be said in public places, it is also worthwhile to be understood in public places. When the cohesive principle of 'united we stand; divided we fall' improves security in the air, there is similarly a strong liklihood it can improve safety, security and progress for all public participants on the ground, as well.

Minority Language Educational Rights

In Canada, people ordinarily have the opportunity to be taught in either the English language or the French language, usually depending on the language previously used in Canada for teaching their parents. Section 23 of the Charter describes that if parents have been taught with using English then their children are typically expected to be taught in English as well. Similarly, when parents have been taught in French, their children can also expect to be taught in French (Canada's only other official public language). Many countries in the world have only one official language; England: English, France: French, Spain: Spanish, etc. Canada, however, recognizes traditional communication and educational methods for the majority of its people in two official languages only: English and French. Rather than producing dissention and confrontation among Canada's two major historic languages and areas of people, Canadian Charter laws officially protect both languages. The primary intention here is to have peaceful communications among Canadians, along with respect and consideration for each other. However, in the area of Canadian aviation, only one official language is used: English. When demonstrable public harm is involved, it is accepted that safety is improved with less confusion and ignorance. Keeping it simple can save lives. Incomplete or misunderstood information are dangerous things tending to produce confusions, delusions, and demonstrable harms.

The Notwithstanding Clause

Section 33 of the Charter provides a temporary override feature for provincial government(s) involvement. What this means is, "that the fundamental freedoms (expression, religion, association and assembly) are subject to being overridden by legislative decision, as are the legal rights and, subject to section 28, the right to equality... These declarations can be in effect for a maximum of five years."[57]

This temporary override clause (the Notwithstanding Clause) allows flexibility to be inherent in legal processes, providing no related harm is produced.

In summary, the override clause allows the majority of each province or territory, "a legal mechanism to have its way, but it may well be that the people will rarely, if ever, assume the moral burden of overriding protected rights and freedoms."[58] It's nice to know it's there, but only if improvement is for the public good with no arbitrary demonstrable harm(s) to any person or property.

Enforcement

Any citizen of Canada whose right(s), freedom(s), person or property(ies) are harmfully affected, "is entitled to raise a constitutional issue in a civil proceeding or by way of defence to a criminal prosecution."[59] Section 24(1) of the Charter specifically proclaims that, "Anyone whose rights or freedoms, as guaranteed by this Charter, have been infringed or denied may appeal to a court of competent jurisdiction to obtain such remedy as the court considers appropriate and just in the circumstances."[60] In addition, "there seems no reason in principle why compensatory damages should not be available where the injured party can establish a loss, capable of measurement in money terms, that was caused by the Charter breach."[61]

Citation

A general beneficial intention of the Charter is to provide people in Canada with principles and actions that add value and give immeasureable joy. Section 34 legally stipulates, "We must now establish the basic principles, the basic values and beliefs which hold us together as Canadians so that beyond our regional loyalties there is a way of life and a system of values which make us proud of the country that has given us such freedom and immeasureable joy."[62]

Conclusion

The Canadian Charter of Rights and Freedoms provides an abundance of personal and public protections encouraging everyone to add value to society rather than produce harm. "The Charter contains only those rights and freedoms that Canadians believe are essential in a free and democratic country. They have been set out in the Constitution as a way of making sure that they are given the greatest protection possible under the law."[63]

In addition, "The Charter represents a restatement of the fundamental values which guide and shape our democratic society and our legal system. It follows that it is appropriate for the courts to make such incremental revisions to the common law as may be necessary to have it comply with the values being enunciated in the Charter."[64] Liberty, equality, security and joy are included in such essential fundamental principles that promote peace, order and prosperity for all helpful participants.

Since the comprehensive and cohesive Canadian Charter of Rights and Freedoms legally came into force in 1982, "legislatures cannot enact laws without consideration of their legal impact on individual rights, and governmental officers play an important role..."[65] More specifically, all laws, statutes, regulations and courts are subject to Charter scrutiny as are actions of the police, including any and all officers and other governmental personnel, in their treatment of individuals. Canada must be a just society, that helps its nonharmful people.

Perhaps the hospitable words of Canada's peace promoting prime minister, Jean Cretien provide further inspiration and hope for a successful future. "After 115 years as a nation, Canadians turned our shared values into a document which serves as the guiding law of our land and entrenches the liberties of all of us who call Canada home."[66] Guaranteed rights and freedoms to live and add value in a fair, joyful, and peaceful democracy are general and popular purposes of the Canadian Charter of Rights and Freedoms. Everyone should have pleasant things to look forward to, not involving harm to others or their property.

THE CANADIAN CHARTER OF RIGHTS AND FREEDOMS

April 17, 1982 is an historic date in the development of Canadian human rights and freedoms. On this day, Canada officially proclaimed its new and most prominent level of laws in the country, the guaranteed and democratically valuable Canadian Charter of Rights and Freedoms. Canada's federal government, with skillful leadership from Pierre Elliott Trudeau, designed and described the legal contents of these significant Canadian laws, that now override all other laws in Canada, including all municipal and provincial statutes. It was the first time in history that so many important constitutional laws were legally put into force for protecting nonharmful individuals in Canada. Also, this Charter of guaranteed rights and freedoms can only be legally changed by majority-vote from the Canadian House of Commons, with additional approval by majority-vote of the Canadian Senate, along with further approval from designated provincial government participants. As a consequence, any amendment(s) are not likely to include quick and secretive change(s). Democracy both for the people and for each person is abundantly provided in this charter. Canadians can feel proud in presently having the fairest and most comprehensive charter of rights and freedoms in the world.

The complete contents of the Canadian Charter of Rights and Freedoms are exactly as follows:

"Whereas Canada is founded upon principles that recognize the supremecy of God and the rule of law:

Guarantee of Rights and Freedoms

1. The Canadian Charter of Rights and Freedoms guarantees the rights and freedoms set out in it subject only to such reasonable limits prescribed by law as can be demonstrably justified in a free and democratic society.

Fundamental Freedoms

2. Everyone has the following fundamental freedoms:
    (a) freedom of conscience and religion;
    (b) freedom of thought, belief, opinion and expression,
        including freedom of the press and other media of
        communication;
    (c) freedom of peaceful assembly; and
    (d) freedom of association.

Democratic Rights

3. Every citizen of Canada has the right to vote in an election of
   members of the House of Commons or of a legislative
   assembly and to be qualified for membership therein.

4. (1) No House of Commons and no legislative
       assembly shall continue for longer than five
       years from the date fixed for the return of writs
       at a general election of its members.

   (2) In time of real or apprehended war, invasion or
       insurrection, a House of Commons may be continued
       by Parliament and a legislative assembly may be
       continued by the legislature beyond five years
       if such continuation is not opposed by the votes of more
       than one-third of the members of the House of Commons
       or the legislative assembly, as the case may be.

5. There shall be a sitting of Parliament and of each
   legislature at least once every twelve months.

Mobility Rights

6. (1) Every citizen of Canada has the right to enter, remain
       in and leave Canada.
   (2) Every citizen of Canada and every person who
       has the status of a permanent resident has the right

6. (2) (a) to move to and take up residence in any province, and to pursue the gaining of a livlihood.

6. (3) The rights specified in subsection (2) are subject to

(a) any laws or practices of general application in force in a province other than those that discriminate persons primarily on the basis of province of present or previous residence; and

(b) any laws providing for reasonable residence requirements as a qualification for the receipt of publicly provided social services.

6. (4) Subsections (2) and (3) do not preclude any law, program or activity that has as its object the amelioration in a province of conditions of individuals in that province who are socially or economically disadvantaged if the rate of employment in that province is below the rate of employment in Canada.

Legal Rights

7. Everyone has the right to life, liberty and security of the person and the right not to be deprived thereof except in accordance with the principles of fundamental justice.

8. Everyone has the right to be secure against unreasonable search or seizure.

9. Everyone has the right not to be arbitrarily detained or imprisoned.

10. Everyone has the right on arrest or detention
(a) to be informed promptly of the reasons therefore;
(b) to retain and instruct counsel without delay and to be informed of that right; and
(c) to have the validity of the detention determined by way of habeus corpus and to be released if the detention is not lawful.

11. Any person charged with an offence has the right
   (a) to be informed without unreasonable delay of the specific offence;
   (b) to be tried within a reasonable time;
   (c) not to be compelled to be a witness in proceedings against that person in respect of the offence.
   (d) to be presumed innocent until proven guilty according to law in a fair and public hearing by an independant and impartial tribunal;
   (e) not to be denied reasonable bail without just cause;
   (f) except in the case of an offence under military law tried before a military tribunal, to the benefit of trial by jury where the maximum punishment for the offence is imprisonment for five years or a more severe punishment;
   (g) not to be found guilty on account of any act or omission unless, at the time of the act or omission, it constituted an offence under Canadian or international law or was criminal according to the general principles of law recognized by the community of nations;
   (h) if finally acquitted of the offence, not to be tried for it again and, if finally found guilty and punished for the offence, not to tried or punished for it again; and
   (i) if found guilty of the offence and if the punishment for the offence has been varied between the time of commission and the time of sentencing, to the benefit of the lesser punishment.

12. Everyone has the right not to be subjected to any cruel and unusual treatment or punishment.

13. A witness who testifies in any proceedings has the right not to have any incriminating evidence so given used to incriminate that witness in any other proceedings, except in a prosecution for perjury or for the giving of contradictory evidence.

14. A party or witness in any proceedings who does not understand or speak the language in which the proceedings are conducted or who is deaf has the the right to the assistance of an interpreter.

Equality Rights

15. (1) Every individual is equal before and under the law and has the right to the equal protection and equal benefit of the law without discrimination, and in particular, without discrimination based on race, national or ethnic origin, colour, religion, sex, age, or mental or physical disability.

    (2) Subsection (1) does not preclude any law, program or activity that has as its object the amelioration of conditions of disadvantaged individuals or groups including those that are disadvantaged because of race, national or ethnic origin, colour, religion, sex, age, or mental or physical disability.

Official Languages of Canada

16. (1) English and French are the official languages of Canada and have equality of status and equal rights and priveleges as to their use in all institutions of the Parliament and government of Canada.

    (2) English and French are the official languages of New Brunswick and have equality of status and equal rights and priveleges as to their use in all institutions of the legislature and government of New Brunswick.

    (3) Nothing in this Charter limits the authority of Parliament or a legislature to advance the equality of status or use of English and French.

17. (1) Everyone has the right to use English or French in any debates and other proceedings of Parliament.

(2) Everyone has the right to use English or French in any debates and other proceedings of the legislature of New Brunswick.

18. (1) The statutes, records and journals of Parliament shall be printed and published in English and French and both language versions are equally authoritative.

(2) The statutes, records and journals of the legislature of New Brunswick shall be printed and published in English and French and both language versions are equally authoritative.

19. (1) Either English or French may be used by any person in, or in any pleading in or process issuing from, any court established by Parliament.

(2) Either English or French may be used by any person in, or in any pleading in or processs issuing from, any court of New Brunswick.

20. (1) Any member of the public in Canada has the right to communicate with, and to receive available services from, any head or central office of an institution of the Parliament or government of Canada in English or French, and has the same right with respect to any other office of any such institution where
(a) there is a significant demand for communications with and services from that office in such language; or
(b) due to the nature of the office, it is reasonable that communications with and services from that office be available in both English and French.

20. (2) Any member of the public in New Brunswick has the right to communicate with, and to receive available services from, any office of an institution of the legislature or government of New Brunswick in English or French.

21. Nothing in sections 16 to 20 abrogates or derogates from any right, privelege or obligation with respect to the English and French languages, or either of them, that exists or is continued by virtue of any other provision of the Constitution of Canada.

22. Nothing in sections 16 to 20 abrogates or derogates from any legal or customary right or privelege acquired or enjoyed either before or after the coming into force of this Charter with respect to any language that is not English or French.

<u>Minority Language Educational Rights</u>

23. (1) Citizens of Canada
   (a) whose first language learned and still understood is that of the English or French linguistic minority population of the province in which they reside, or
   (b) who have received their primary school instruction in Canada in English or French and reside in a province where the language in which they received that instruction is the language of English or French linguistic minority population of the province, and secondary school instruction in the same language.
   (2) Citizens of Canada whom any child has received or is receiving primary or secondary school instruction in English or French in Canada, have the right to have all their children receive primary and secondary school instruction in the same language.

23. (3) The right of citizens of Canada under subsections (1) and (2) to have their children receive primary and secondary school instruction in the language of the English or French linguistic minority population of a province
   (a) applies wherever in the province the number of

children of citizens who have such a right is
sufficient to warrant the provision to them
out of public funds of minority language
instruction; and

23. (3) (b) includes, where the number of those children so
warrants, the right to have them receive that
instruction in minority language educational
facilities provided out of public funds.

Enforcement

24. (1) anyone whose rights or freedoms, as guaranteed by
this Charter, have been infringed or denied may
apply to a court of competent jurisdiction to
obtain such remedy as the court considers
appropriate and just in the circumstances.

(2) Where, in proceedings under subsection (1), a
court concludes that evidence was obtained in
a manner that infringed or denied any rights
or freedoms guaranteed by this Charter, the
evidence shall be excluded if it is established
that, having regard to all the circumstances,
the admission of it in the proceedings would
bring the administration of justice into disrepute.

General

25. The guarantee in this Charter of certain rights and
freedoms shall not be construed so as to abrogate
or derogate from any aboriginal treaty or other rights
or freedoms that pertain to the aboriginal peoples
of Canada including

(a) any rights or freedoms that have been recognized
by the Royal Proclamation of October 7, 1763; and

(b) any rights or freedoms that may be acquired by the
aboriginal peoples of Canada by way of land claims
settlement.

26. The guarantee in this Charter of certain rights and
freedoms shall not be construed as denying the
existance of any other rights and freedoms that exist
in Canada.

27. This Charter shall be interpreted in a manner consistent
with the preservation and enhancement of the
multicultural heritage of Canadians.

28. Notwithstanding anything in this Charter, the rights and
freedoms referred to in it are guaranteed equally to
male and female persons.

29. Nothing in this Charter abrogates or derogates from any
rights or priveleges guaranteed by or under the
Constitution of Canada in respect of denominational,
separate or dissentient schools.

30. A reference in this Charter to a province or to the
legislative assembly or legislature of a province shall
be deemed to include a reference to the Yukon Territory
and the Northwest Territories, or to the appropriate
legislative authority thereof, as the case may be.

31. Nothing in this Charter extends the legislative powers
of any body or authority.

Application of Charter

32. (1) This Charter applies
        (a) to the Parliament and government of Canada
            in respect of all matters within the authority
            of Parliament including all matters relating to
            the Yukon Territory and Northwest Territories; and

        (b) to the legislature and government of each province
            in respect of all matters within the authority of
            the legislature of each province.

32. (2) Notwithstanding subsection (1), section 15 shall not
have effect until three years after this section
comes into force.

33. (1) Parliament or the legislature of a province may
expressly declare in an Act of Parliament or
of the legislature, as the case may be, that the Act
or a provision thereof shall operate notwithstanding
a provision included in section 2 or sections 7 to 15
of this Charter.

(2) An Act or a provision of an Act in respect of which a
declaration made under this section is in effect
shall have such operation as it would have but
for the provision of this Charter referred to in
the declaration.

(3) A declaration made under subsection (1) shall cease
to have effect five years after it comes into force
or on such earlier date as may be specified in
the declaration.

(4) Parliament or a legislature of a province may re-enact
a declaration made under subsection (1).

(5) Subsection (3) applies in respect of a re-enactment
made under subsection (4).

Citation

34. This part may be cited as the Canadian Charter of Rights
and Freedoms.

"We must now establish the basic principles, the basic
values and beliefs which hold us together as Canadians
so that beyond our regional loyalties there is a way
of life and a system of values which make us proud
of the country that has given us such freedom and
such immeasurable joy."[67]

GLOSSARY OF TERMS

Aboriginal: the first people to live in a region since the beginning of recorded history.

Abrogate: to abolish, annul or revoke previously approved obligations.

Acquit: to clear a person of a charge, or to release a person from an obligation.

Aesthetic: relating to beauty and art.

Affiliation: associating oneself with a group.

Affirmative: confirming or agreeing with, or to positively support.

Amelioration: an improved situation, or things made better.

Amendment: a revision to a statute or law.

Arbitrary: action(s) based on whim, or another person's preference.

Arrest: to seize with authority of the law, or to legally remove liberty rights from a person.

Arrogant: demonstrating a superiority attitude, or being vain and selfish.

Assembly: a group of three or more people gathered together.

Association: a collection of persons with the same or similar purpose(s).

Attain: to accomplish or achieve.

Aversion: an intense dislike for something(s).

Bail: money deposited with a court to have a person temporarily released from jail.

Belief: a confidence or reliable understanding that a certain thing is true.

Benefit: anything contributing to an improvement.

Bonding: a provision of security authorizing future activities of a person.

Breach: a failure to observe a law, promise or agreement.

Citizen: a person who is born in a country, or receives official status of citizen through specified government procedures.

Civil: private legal matter(s) including contract(s) and other wrongful acts (torts) that are not of a criminal offence nature.

Coercion: any form of constraint or compulsion which induces a person to act otherwise than freely. It is usually mental pressure brought to bear on a person's freewill.

Collective Good: of benefit to the general public.

Colloquial: informal or casual communication.

Common Law: laws based on customs and judicial decisions.

Compel: to force or coerce.

Compulsion: applying force against a person's free will.

Conscience: a sense of right and wrong, relating to harmful and beneficial actions.

Constitution: a governmental description of basic laws and principles for a country.

Constitutional Issue: violation of a constitutional provision that could involve court proceedings.

Construe: to explain or interpret.

Counsel: to advise or recommend, or a lawyer or a group of lawyers.

Criminal Code: laws relating to the criminal justice system.

Criminal Offence: an indictable offence violating an act of parliament.

Criminal Procedure: laws relating to the process of the criminal justice system.

Criminal Record: a summary of a person's contacts with law enforcement, including arrests, convictions and sentences.

Defence: introduction of evidence in court designed to refute part or all of the allegations made against a person.

Demonstrable: that which can be demonstrated or proved.

Demonstrable Harm: substantiated and proven damage or injury to a person or property.

Demonstrable Justification: proven, identifiable and measureable harm must be produced before guilt and punishment are legally allowed to be pronounced and enforced.

Denominational (School): with religious background and operational control.

Derogate: to reduce, diminish or decrease.

Detain: to delay, keep or restrain.

Deviate: to turn away or diverge from, or to act contrary to expected behaviour.

Dignity: showing honourable quality and worthiness.

Disrepute: disgraceful or bad reputation.

Dissemination: to spread or communicate widely.

Dissentient: disagreeing with an official or majority view.

Endeavour: to make an earnest attempt, or to try with much effort.

Enhancement: to improve with quality or quantity.

Equal: of the same value, or having the same rights and and strengths.

Equality: having the same legal rights and freedoms.

Ermine: valuable white animal fur, emblematic of purity and fairness.

Faculty: a natural or specialized power or aptitude.

Freedom: exemption from obligation, discomfort or or inconvenience, or independence to do nonharmful action(s).

Fundamental Justice: principles relating to fairness. Also, being fully informed of an offence supposedly committed; giving the accused a fair opportunity to present a case, with having knowledge of any related evidence, and with corresponding judicial decisions determined using materials properly presented in court.

Good (Collective): action(s) intended to improve benefit(s) for at least the majority of people involved (same as public good).

Guarantee: an assurance that something will perform, or be administered or done as previously specified.

Habeas Corpus: the right to trial within a reasonable time; or, a legal requirement that a detained person be soon brought before a court to determine the legality of the detention.

Happiness: showing or causing great pleasure or joy.

Harm: to hurt, injure, damage or malign.

Hate Speech: communucation(s) involving ill will, fear or intimidation to a person(s) or group because of race, colour, religion, ethnic origin, sex, age, or mental or physical disability.

Heritage: tradition that continues from one generation to the next.

Hospitable: being friendly while showing abundant care and concern to those immediately involved.

Inclination: a preference or tendency for something.

Incremental: a recent increase or change.

Incriminate: to involve, or make appear guilty of a demonstrable harm or crime.

Indictable: a criminal offence against a federal act or law of parliament.

Induce: to persuade, convince, or win over; or, to draw a conclusion from existing facts.

Infringe: to intrude or encroach on the rights or freedoms of others; or to breach a law or agreement.

Innate: natural, inborn, fundamental and true.

Innocent: harmless, free from evil, or not guilty of a specified crime.

Insurrection: a violent uprising by part or all of the people against a government or other established authority; a rebellion.

Joy: a very delightful, pleasant or happy feeling.

Jurisdiction: range of authority for administering justice; the legal power to hear and determine a case.

Just Cause: such reason(s) as would justify removal of specific legal right(s) because of previous proven related harm produced; or, detrimental violation of an agreement. An example is losing the legal right to own or use any firearm because of a previous proven conviction of unprovoked murder by using a firearm. Also, habitual neglect by an employee in correctly following approved safety procedures adversely affecting lives and limbs of others exemplifies a detrimental violation of agreement, resulting in the legal right or 'just cause' to dismiss such an employee.

Legislative Assembly: the official democratically elected government (legislature) of a province or territory.

Libel: any written or printed information that unjustly harms a person's reputation.

Liberty: freedom to do nonharmful action(s); ability to make use of all rights and freedoms specified in a country's constitution.

Life: one's existance of being alive.

Linguistic: the study or analysis of a particular language.

Majority: more than half of the true total; fifty percent plus
       at least one.

Media: any and all methods of communication including
       newspapers, televisions, radios, computers, etc.

Minority: less than half; a smaller disadvantaged group that has
       common differences than the larger controlling group.

Mobility: legal freedom and ability to move anywhere in the
       country, particularly for obtaining employment.

Momentous: a great and very important moment in history.

Morals: in accordance with right and wrong; good in conduct,
       attitude and behaviour.

Notion: a general idea including a belief or opinion.

Notwithstanding: irrespective of, in spite of, in any case.

Objective: purpose, aim or goal; concerned with realities.

Opinion: a belief about what seems to be true or very probable.

Order: the preservation of all kinds and amounts of good which
       already exist; to sort out, arrange, sequentialize, or
       organize.

Parliament: the House of Commons and the Senate of the
       Canadian federal government.

Perjury: willfilly telling a lie while under oath; intending to
       mislead by making a false statement(s) while under
       oath.

Permanent Resident: a person who: 1) has received lawful permission to come into Canada; 2) is not a Canadian citizen; and 3) has not ceased having the legal description of permanent resident as per subsection 24(1) of the Canadian Immigration Act.

Posterity: all future generations' lives.

Preservation: protection from harm(s).

Principle: a fundamental truth upon which other truths are based.

Privelege: a special favour or right granted to a person or group.

Proceeding: an action, matter or cause before a court (civil or criminal).

Proclamation: an official announcement or publication.

Progress: an increase in the preservation of all kinds and amounts of good; an improvement or moving forward towards a successful completion.

Proof: evidence that establishes the truth of something.

Prosecution (Criminal): the putting of an alleged offender on trial for violating a federal or provincial act, statute or law.

Protection: a defence, guard or shield from harm or danger.

Public Good: action(s) that improve benefits for all in general.

Punishment: imposing a loss or penalty for being guilty of an unlawful offence.

Religion: a specific system of beliefs and worship, often including a code of ethics with a belief in, and praise for God.

Reputation: a favourable estimation in which a person or thing is commonly held.

Residence: a place where a person lives or dwells.

Respect: to show consideration, courtesy and politeness for.

Right: power, freedom and privelege belonging to one by law.

Royal Proclamation of October 7, 1763: a British government agreement identifying land, resources, and related treaty rights for aboriginal people in Eastern and Western Canada.

Scrutiny: a close examination for truth.

Security: freedom from fear of being harmed; a protection or safeguard.

Separate (School): private school usually operated by and for Roman Catholics.

Slander: verbally saying something false (particularly in public) that harms or damages another person's reputation.

Statute: an established rule or law passed by a legislative authority.

Submit: to offer as an opinion; to present to others for their consideration; to yield to the power or control of another person(s).

Thought: the power of reasoning with ideas and concepts.

Treatment: action(s) involving method(s) or procedure(s) intended for improvement(s).

Treaty: a formal understanding and agreement between at least two nations.

Tribunal: a legal court of justice.

Validity: based on truthful evidence or logical reasoning; having legal force.

Value: a thing(s) of quality regarded as being useful, worthwhile and desirable by others.

Warrant (To): to justify for specific actions.

Willful: said or done deliberately.

Worship: a service or solemn ceremony showing reverence, admiration and respect.

FOOTNOTES

1. <u>World Book Encyclopedia</u> <u>Volume 19(T)</u> Toronto: World Book, 2002. p.463.

2. Ibid. p.463.

3. Minister of Public Works and Government Services, Human Rights Program, Department of Canadian Heritage, <u>Your Guide to the Canadian Charter of Rights and Freedoms,</u> Hull, Canada: 1997. Introduction.

4. Ibid. p.1.

5. Trudeau, Pierre Elliott <u>Canadian Charter of Rights and Freedoms,</u> Ottawa: Government of Canada, 1981. p.1.

6. Sharpe, R.J. and Swinton, K.E. <u>The Charter of Rights and Freedoms,</u> Toronto: Irwin Law, 1998. p.31.

7. Mill, John Stuart (Edited by: McCallum, R.B.) <u>On Liberty and Considerations on Representative Government,</u> (Originally From England: 1861) Oxford: Basil Blackwell, 1948. p.x.

8. Locke, John (Edited by: Macpherson, C.B.) <u>Second Treatise of Government,</u> (Originally from England: 1690) Indiana: Hackett Publishing Co. Inc., 1980. p.xi.

9. Bentham, Jeremy (Edited by: Hart H.) <u>The Collected Works of Jeremy Bentham,</u> <u>Of Laws in General,</u> <u>Principles of Legislation,</u> (Originally from England: 1789) London: The Athlone Press, 1970. p.289.

10. Mill, John Stuart (Edited by: McCallum, R.B.) <u>On Liberty and Considerations on Representative Government,</u>

(Originally from England: 1861) Oxford: Basil Blackwell,
pp.8 and 11.

11. Trudeau, Pierre Elliott <u>Canadian Charter of Rights and
Freedoms</u>, Ottawa: Government of Canada, 1981. p.1.

12. Sharpe, R.J. and Swinton, K.E. The <u>Charter of Rights and
Freedoms</u>, Toronto: Irwin Law, 1998. p.154.

13. Ibid. p.154.

14. Fine, Ralph Adam <u>Mary Jane Versus Pennsylvania</u>,
New York: The McCall Publishing Co., 1970. p.9.

15. Meehan, E. Cuddy, K.M. Elkin, C. Fairley, H.S. Fera, N. et al
<u>The 2000 Annotated Canadian Charter of Rights and
Freedoms</u>, Ontario: Carswell Thomas Professional
Publishing, 1999. p.437.

16. Trudeau, Pierre Elliott <u>Canadian Charter of Rights and
Freedoms</u>, Ottawa: Government of Canada, 1981. p.1.

17. Ibid. p.1.

18. Ibid. p.1.

19. Meehan, E. Cuddy, K.M. Elkin, C. Fairley, H.S. Fera, N. et al
<u>The 2000 Annotated Canadian Charter of Rights and
Freedoms</u>, Ontario: Carswell Thomas Professional
Publishing, 1999. p.437.

20. Mill, John Stuart (Edited by: McCallum, R.B.) <u>On Liberty
and Considerations on Representative Government</u>,
(Originally from England: 1861) Oxford: Basil Blackwell,
1948. p.121.

21. Meehan, E. Cuddy, K.M. Elkin, C. Fairley, H.S. Fera, N. et al
<u>The 2000 Annotated Canadian Charter of Rights and
Freedoms</u>, Ontario: Carswell T. Professional Publishing,
1999. p.74.

22. Gifis, Steven H. <u>Law Dictionary</u> <u>Fourth Edition</u>, New York: Baron's Educational Series Inc., 1996. p.83.

23. Meehan, E. Cuddy, K.M. Elkin, C. Fairley, H.S. Fera, N. et al <u>The 2000 Annotated Canadian Charter of Rights and Freedoms</u>, Ontario: Carswell Thomas Professional Publishing, 1999. p.89.

24. Mill, John Stuart (Edited by: McCallum, R.B.) <u>On Liberty and Considerations on Representative Government</u>, (Originally from England: 1861) Oxford: Basil Blackwell, 1948. p.11.

25. Ibid. p.17.

26. Minister of Public Works and Government Services, <u>Human Rights Program, Department of Canadian Heritage, Your Guide to the Canadian Charter of Rights and Freedoms</u>, Hull, Canada: 1997. Introduction.

27. Mill, John Stuart (Edited by: McCallum, R.B.) <u>On Liberty and Considerations on Representative Government</u>, (Originally from England: 1861) Oxford: Basil Blackwell, 1948. p.16.

28. Ibid. p.57.

29. Ibid. p.57.

30. Ibid. pp.14-15.

31. Sharpe, R.J. and Swinton, K.E. <u>The Charter of Rights and Freedoms</u>, Toronto: Irwin Law, 1998. p.102.

32. Ibid. p.92.

33. Meehan, E. Cuddy, K.M. Elkin, C. Fairley, H.S. Fera, N. et al <u>The 2000 Annotated Canadian Charter of Rights and Freedoms</u>, Ontario: Carswell Thomas Professional Publishing, 1999. p.138.

34. Gifis, Steven H. <u>Law Dictionary</u> <u>Fourth Edition</u>, New York: Baron's Educational Series Inc., 1996. p.535.

35. Ibid. p.35.

36. Ibid. p.35.

37. Meehan, E. Cuddy, K.M. Elkin, C. Fairley, H.S. Fera, N. et al <u>The 2000 Annotated Canadian Charter of Rights and Freedoms</u>, Ontario: Carswell Thomas Professional Publishing, 1999. p.139.

38. Ibid. p.139.

39. Mill, John Stuart (Edited by: McCallum, R.B.) <u>On Liberty and Considerations on Representative Government</u>, (Originally from England: 1861) Oxford: Basil Blackwell, 1948. p.11.

40. Trudeau, Pierre Elliott <u>Canadian Charter of Rights and Freedoms</u>, Ottawa: Government of Canada, p.1.

41. Gifis, Steven H. <u>Law Dictionary</u> <u>Fourth Edition</u>, New York: Baron's Educational Series Inc., 1996. p.121.

42. Ibid. p.121.

43. Hobbes, Thomas (Edited by: Tuck, R.) <u>Leviathan</u> <u>Cambridge Texts in the History of Political Thought</u>, (Originally from England: 1651) Cambridge University Press, 1996. pp.86-87.

44. Locke, John (Edited by: Macpherson, C.B.) <u>Second Treatise of Government</u>, (Originally from England: 1690) Indiana: Hackett Publishing Co. Inc., 1980. p.xiii.

45. Trudeau, Pierre Elliott <u>Canadian Charter of Rights and Freedoms</u>, Ottawa: Government of Canada, 1981. p.1.

46. Meehan, E. Cuddy, K.M. Elkin, C. Fairley, H.S. Fera, N. et al
The 2000 Annotated Canadian Charter of Rights and
Freedoms, Ontario: Carswell Thomas Professional
Publishing, 1999. p.638.

47. Ibid. p.638.

48. Trudeau, Pierre Elliott Canadian Charter of Rights and
Freedoms, Ottawa: Government of Canada, 1981. p.1.

49. Sharpe, R.J. and Swinton K.E. The Charter of Rights and
Freedoms, Toronto: Irwin Law, 1998. p.186.

50. Ibid. p.184.

51. Trudeau, Pierre Elliott Canadian Charter of Rights and
Freedoms, Ottawa: Government of Canada, 1981. p.1.

52. Ibid p.1.

53. Sharpe, R.J. and Swinton, K.E. The Charter of Rights and
Freedoms, Toronto: Irwin Law: 1998. pp.131-132.

54. Trudeau, Pierre Elliott Canadian Charter of Rights and
Freedoms, Ottawa: Government of Canada, 1981. p.1.

55. Sharpe, R.J. and Swinton, K.E. The Charter of Rights and
Freedoms, Toronto: Irwin Law, 1998. p.210.

56. Trudeau, Pierre Elliott Canadian Charter of Rights and
Freedoms, Ottawa: Government of Canada, 1981. p.1.

57. Sharpe, R.J. and Swinton, K.E. The Charter of Rights and
Freedoms, Toronto: Irwin Law, 1998. pp.54-55.

58. Ibid. p.57.

59. Ibid. p.69.

60. Trudeau, Pierre Elliott <u>Canadian Charter of Rights and Freedoms</u>, Ottawa: Government of Canada, 1981. p.1.

61. Sharpe, R.J. and Swinton, K.E. <u>The Charter of Rights and Freedoms</u>, Toronto: Irwin Law, 1998. p.220.

62. Trudeau, Pierre Elliott <u>Canadian Charter of Rights and Freedoms</u>, Ottawa: Government of Canada, 1981. p.1.

63. Minister of Public Works and Government Services, Human Rights Program, Department of Canadian Heritage, <u>Your Guide to the Canadian Charter of Rights and Freedoms</u>, Hull, Canada: 1997. p.2.

64. Sharpe, R.J. and Swinton, K.E. <u>The Charter of Rights and Freedoms</u>, Toronto: Irwin Law, 1998. p.65.

65. Ibid. p.28.

66. Minister of Public Works and Government Services, Human Rights Program, Department of Canadian Heritage, <u>Your Guide to the Canadian Charter of Rights and Freedoms</u>, Hull, Canada: 1997. Foreward.

67. Trudeau, Pierre Elliott <u>Canadian Charter of Rights and Freedoms</u>, Ottawa: Government of Canada, 1981. p.1.

BIBLIOGRAPHY

BENTHAM, JEREMY (Edited by: Hart, H.) <u>The Collected Works of Jeremy Bentham</u>, <u>Of Laws in General</u>, <u>Principles of Legislation</u>, (Originally from England: 1789) London: The Athlone Press, 1970.

<u>CANADIAN LAW DICTIONARY</u>, Adapted from: Gifis, Steven H. New York: Baron's Educational Series Inc., 2003.

DUKELOW, DAPHNE A. and NUSE, BETSY The <u>Dictionary of Canadian Law</u>, Scarborough, Ontario: Thompson Professional Publishing Canada, 1991.

FINE, RALPH ADAM <u>Mary Jane Versus Pennsylvania</u>, New York: The McCall Publishing Company, 1970.

GIFIS, STEVEN H. <u>Law Dictionary</u> <u>Fourth Edition</u>, New York: Baron's Educational Series Inc., 1996.

HOBBES, THOMAS (Edited by: Tuck, R.) <u>Leviathan</u>, (Originally from England: 1651) Cambridge: University Press, 1996.

HOGUE, ARTHUR R. <u>Origins of the Common Law</u>, Indianapolis: Liberty Press, 1985.

LOCKE, JOHN (Edited by: Macpherson, C.B.) <u>Second Treatise of Government</u>, (Originally from England: 1690) Indiana: Hackett Publishing Co. Inc. 1980.

MEEHAN, E. CUDDY, K. ELKIN, C. FAIRLEY, H. FERA, N. et al. <u>The 2000 Annotated Canadian Charter of Rights and Freedoms</u>, Ontario: Carswell Thomas Professional Publishing, 1999.

MILL, JOHN STUART (Edited by: McCallum, R.B.) <u>On Liberty and Considerations on Representative Government</u>, (Originally from England: 1861) Oxford: Basil Blackwell, 1948.

MINISTER OF PUBLIC WORKS AND GOVERNMENT SERVICES, HUMAN RIGHTS PROGRAM, DEPARTMENT OF CANADIAN HERITAGE, Your Guide to the Canadian Charter of Rights and Freedoms, Hull, Canada: 1997.

SHARPE, R.J. and SWINTON, K.E. The Charter of Rights and Freedoms, Toronto: Irwin Law, 1998.

THE CANADIAN OXFORD DICTIONARY, (Edited by: Barber, K.) Oxford: University Press, 1998.

TRUDEAU, PIERRE ELLIOTT Canadian Charter of Rights and Freedoms, Ottawa: Government of Canada, 1981.

WEBSTER'S NEW WORLD DICTIONARY AND THESAURUS, (Edited by: Agnes, Michael) New York: Macmillan, 1996.

WORLD BOOK ENCYCLOPEDIA VOLUME 19 (T) Toronto: World Book, 1992.

INDEX

Printed in the United States
by Baker & Taylor Publisher Services